Better Homes and Gardens®

Easy Stir-Fry Recipes

Our seal assures you that every recipe in *Easy Stir-Fry Recipes*
has been tested in the Better Homes and Gardens® Test Kitchen.
This means that each recipe is practical and reliable,
and meets our high standards of taste appeal.

BETTER HOMES AND GARDENS® BOOKS

Editor: Gerald M. Knox
Art Director: Ernest Shelton
Managing Editor: David A. Kirchner
Editorial Project Managers: James D. Blume, Marsha Jahns,
    Rosanne Weber Mattson

Department Head, Cook Books: Sharyl Heiken
Associate Department Heads: Sandra Granseth,
    Rosemary C. Hutchinson, Elizabeth Woolever
Senior Food Editors: Linda Henry, Marcia Stanley,
    Joyce Trollope
Associate Food Editors: Mary Major, Diana McMillen,
    Mary Jo Plutt, Linda Foley Woodrum
Test Kitchen: Director, Sharon Stilwell; Photo Studio Director,
    Janet Herwig; Home Economists: Jean Brekke, Kay Cargill,
    Marilyn Cornelius, Jennifer Darling, Maryellyn Krantz,
    Lynelle Munn, Dianna Nolin, Marge Steenson

Associate Art Directors: Linda Ford Vermie, Neoma Thomas,
    Randall Yontz
Assistant Art Directors: Lynda Haupert, Harijs Priekulis,
    Tom Wegner
Graphic Designers: Mary Schlueter Bendgen, Mike Burns,
    Brian Wignall
Art Production: Director, John Berg; Associate, Joe Heuer;
    Office Manager, Michaela Lester

President, Book Group: Jeramy Lanigan
Vice President, Retail Marketing: Jamie L. Martin
Vice President, Administrative Services: Rick Rundall

BETTER HOMES AND GARDENS® MAGAZINE
President, Magazine Group: James A. Autry
Editorial Director: Doris Eby
Food and Nutrition Editor: Nancy Byal

MEREDITH CORPORATE OFFICERS
Chairman of the Executive Committee: E.T. Meredith III
Chairman of the Board: Robert A. Burnett
President: Jack D. Rehm

EASY STIR-FRY RECIPES

Editor: Diana McMillen
Editorial Project Manager: Marsha Jahns
Contributing Graphic Designer: Patty Konecny
Electronic Text Processor: Paula Forest
Food Stylists: Jennifer Darling, Janet Herwig
Contributing Photographer: Michael Jensen,
    Sean Fitzgerald
Contributing Illustrator: Kate Thomssen

On the cover: *California Stir-Fry*
(see recipe, page 39)

Contents

4 **Make-It-Easy Stir-Fry**
Make a stir-fry for your next meal. It's so easy!

6 **Stir-Fry, American Style**
Favorite American ingredients and sauces in main-dish stir-fries.

34 **It's the Cut That Counts**
A rundown of cutting techniques for easy stir-frying.

36 **Entertaining with a Stir-Fry**
A menu designed to let you stir-fry at the last minute.

42 **Real Chinese Stir-Fries**
Popular Chinese wok dishes you can make at home.

56 **Rice, Rice, Rice**
Rice—from boiled to fried.

60 **Thai and More**
A taste of other Oriental stir-fries—from the Philippines to Vietnam.

64 **Take a Wok**
What's what in woks and skillets.

66 **Stir-Fry Surprises**
Mouth-watering recipes not usually cooked in a wok.

76 **Oriental Ingredients at a Glance**
A glossary of classic Oriental ingredients.

79 **Index**

Make-It-Easy Stir-Fry

Novice stir-fryers and stir-frying pros: Pull out your wok or skillet and start cooking! In minutes you can stir-fry a delicious meal for the family.

Choose from our collection of recipes made with family-favorite ingredients in the American-style section. Or, a menu for entertaining. When you want more typical wok fare, turn to the chapters containing Oriental and Southeast Asian recipes.

As a bonus, you'll find a chapter of surprising recipes you'd never believe came from your wok. Lasagna, stroganoff, and even burgers, all made with the flick of a wrist. When it comes to stir-frying, you'll find recipes to suit every taste in this one easy-to-use book.

Pork and Broccoli Stir-Fry
(See recipe, page 52.)

Stir-fry in three easy steps. First, combine the sauce and set it aside. When you're stir-frying, it'll be ready to add to the wok.

Next, cut up all the other ingredients. Everything should be ready to toss into the wok before you start to stir-fry.

Finally, preheat your wok, then add the oil. When the oil is hot, it's time to stir-fry. Our Test Kitchen recommends stir-frying vegetables before meat. You'll use less oil that way.

Gingerroot-Turkey Stir-Fry

4 teaspoons cornstarch
1 tablespoon sugar
¼ teaspoon dry mustard
⅔ cup chicken broth
3 tablespoons soy sauce
2 tablespoons dry sherry

● For sauce, in a small mixing bowl stir together cornstarch, sugar, and dry mustard. Stir in the chicken broth, soy sauce, and dry sherry. Set aside.

Tiny sticks of gingerroot give this stir-fry a distinctive flavor that complements the sherry-mustard sauce.

1 tablespoon cooking oil
2 cups small cauliflower flowerets
6 green onions, bias sliced
¼ cup gingerroot cut into 1-inch, toothpick-size pieces (1½ ounces)

● Preheat a wok or large skillet over high heat. Add cooking oil. (Add more oil as necessary during stir-frying.)
　Stir-fry cauliflower in hot oil for 2½ minutes. Add onions and gingerroot. Stir-fry for 1½ minutes. Remove from wok.

1 pound turkey breast tenderloin steaks *or* boneless, skinless chicken breasts halves, cut into bite-size pieces

● Add *half* of the turkey to the hot wok or skillet. Stir-fry for 2 to 3 minutes or till turkey is no longer pink. Remove the turkey from the wok.
　Stir-fry the remaining turkey for 2 to 3 minutes. Return all turkey to wok.

1 apple, cored and cut into thin wedges

● Push meat from center of wok or skillet. Stir sauce; add to center of wok. Cook and stir till thickened and bubbly.
　Stir in cauliflower-onion mixture and apple. Heat mixture through. Remove from wok and keep warm.

3 medium zucchini, shredded (about 4 cups) (optional)

● Stir-fry zucchini for 1½ minutes. Arrange on a serving platter. Top with turkey mixture. Serve immediately. Makes 4 servings.

Whiskey-Sauced Turkey

½ cup light cream *or* milk
⅓ cup water
2 tablespoons all-purpose flour
1 teaspoon instant chicken bouillon granules
½ teaspoon dried thyme, crushed
¼ teaspoon pepper

● For sauce, in a small mixing bowl stir together the light cream or milk, water, flour, bouillon, thyme, and pepper. Set sauce mixture aside.

Two tablespoons of whiskey go a long way in this elegant entrée—it's perfectly spiked.

1 tablespoon cooking oil
2 medium carrots, halved lengthwise and thinly sliced
4 green onions, thinly sliced
1 cup sliced fresh mushrooms

● Preheat a wok or large skillet over high heat. Add cooking oil. (Add more oil as necessary during stir-frying.)
 Stir-fry carrots in hot oil for 2 minutes. Add onions and stir-fry 1 minute. Add mushrooms to wok and stir-fry 1 minute more. Remove vegetables from wok.

1 pound turkey breast tenderloin steaks *or* boneless, skinless chicken breast halves, cut into bite-size pieces

● Add *half* of the turkey or chicken to the wok. Stir-fry for 2 to 3 minutes or till done. Remove from wok. Stir-fry remaining turkey for 2 to 3 minutes. Return all meat to wok.

2 tablespoons whiskey
Hot cooked wild *or* regular rice

● Push meat from center of wok. Stir sauce mixture; add to center of wok. Cook and stir till thickened and bubbly. Add vegetable mixture and whiskey. Cook and stir for 1 minute more. Serve stir-fry over rice. Makes 4 servings.

Plan-Ahead Stir-Fry

Whether it's for entertaining or a fast family meal, your last-minute stir-fry is less hassle if you've sliced and chopped ingredients ahead. Up to 24 hours before mealtime, slice the meat and vegetables and combine sauce ingredients.

Refrigerate each ingredient in a separate, airtight container. Pour the sauce mixture in a screw-top jar so you can shake it before using. When you're ready to stir-fry, your ingredients will be, too.

Currant-Sauced Turkey And Carrots

⅓ cup currant jelly
2 tablespoons cold water
2 tablespoons currants *or* snipped raisins
1 tablespoon lemon juice
2 teaspoons cornstarch
1 teaspoon instant chicken bouillon granules

● For sauce, in a small mixing bowl stir together the jelly, water, currants or raisins, lemon juice, cornstarch, and chicken bouillon granules. Set aside.

1 tablespoon cooking oil
1 clove garlic, minced
3 medium carrots, thinly sliced
6 green onions, bias-sliced into 1-inch pieces

● Preheat a wok or large skillet over high heat. Add cooking oil. (Add more oil as necessary during stir-frying.) Stir-fry garlic for 30 seconds.

Add carrots and stir-fry for 2 to 3 minutes. Add green onions and stir-fry for 1 to 2 minutes more or till vegetables are crisp-tender. Remove the cooked vegetables from the wok.

1 pound turkey breast tenderloin steaks *or* boneless, skinless chicken breast halves, cut into bite-size strips

● Add *half* of the turkey or chicken to the wok. Stir-fry for 2 to 3 minutes or till done. Remove from wok. Stir-fry remaining turkey for 2 to 3 minutes. Return all meat to wok.

Hot cooked rice

● Push turkey from center of wok or skillet. Stir sauce mixture; add to center of wok. Cook and stir till sauce mixture is thickened and bubbly.

Add carrot mixture. Cook and stir for 1 minute more. Serve with hot cooked rice. Makes 4 servings.

Like raisins, currants are dried versions of small seedless grapes. They're grown in Greece and California.

Chicken Tarts

1 9-inch folded refrigerated unbaked piecrust	● Unfold unbaked piecrust and roll into a 12-inch circle. Cut four 5-inch circles from pastry. Shape over bottoms of 6-ounce custard cups (see photo, below). Bake in a 450° oven about 10 minutes or till golden. Let cool for 10 minutes on custard cups. Remove from custard cups and invert on individual serving plates.
1 tablespoon cooking oil **2 green onions, sliced** **4 boneless, skinless chicken breast halves, sliced into bite-size strips (about 1 pound)**	● Meanwhile, preheat a wok or large skillet over high heat. Add cooking oil. (Add more oil as necessary during stir-frying.) Stir-fry green onions 5 seconds. Add *half* of the chicken to wok. Stir-fry 2 to 3 minutes or till done. Remove from wok. Stir-fry remaining chicken for 2 to 3 minutes. Remove from wok.
1 8-ounce package frozen green peas and potatoes with cream sauce, thawed **½ cup shredded process Swiss cheese** **⅓ cup milk** **2 tablespoons dry white wine *or* water** **½ teaspoon dried sage, crushed**	● Add thawed vegetable mixture, cheese, milk, dry white wine or water, and sage to wok. Cover and cook for 1 to 2 minutes or till potatoes are tender. Stir in chicken mixture and heat through. Spoon hot chicken mixture into pastry shells. Makes 4 servings.

Here's a stir-fry version of chicken pot pies. It starts with a package of frozen peas and potatoes in sauce combined with Swiss cheese, milk, sage, and a little wine.

For pastry bowls, place the 5-inch circles of dough over inverted custard cups, as shown.

Chili-Beef Salad

1 **pound boneless beef top round steak** *or* **boneless pork**	● Partially freeze beef or pork. Thinly slice, across the grain, into bite-size pieces. Stack slices; cut into thin strips.
3 **tablespoons vinegar** 2 **tablespoons cooking oil** ¼ **teaspoon salt** ¼ **teaspoon pepper**	● For dressing, in a small mixing bowl stir together the vinegar, cooking oil, salt, and pepper. Set aside.
1 **tablespoon cooking oil** 1 **green** *or* **sweet red pepper, cut into ¾-inch squares** 1 **small onion, sliced and separated into rings** 2 **teaspoons chili powder**	● Preheat a wok or large skillet over high heat. Add cooking oil. (Add more oil as necessary during stir-frying.) Stir-fry green pepper in hot oil for 1 minute. Add onion rings and chili powder to wok and stir-fry for 2 minutes more. Remove from wok.
	● Add *half* of the beef to the wok. Stir-fry for 2 to 3 minutes or till done. Remove from wok. Stir-fry the remaining meat for 2 to 3 minutes. Return all meat and the vegetables to wok.
8 **cups torn leaf lettuce** *or* **romaine** 1 **cup sliced fresh mushrooms**	● Add dressing to wok. Heat through. Remove wok from heat. Add torn greens and sliced mushrooms to wok. Toss for 1 minute or till lettuce wilts slightly. Serve immediately. Makes 4 servings.

ATTENTION, TACO SALAD LOVERS: Here's a stir-fry specialty just for you. This salad spiced with chili powder tastes just like that Mexican restaurant favorite.

Hot Bacon and Chicken Salad

⅓ cup Italian salad dressing ¼ teaspoon dry mustard	● For dressing, in a small bowl stir together Italian salad dressing and dry mustard. Set dressing aside.
6 slices bacon, cut crosswise into fourths	● Preheat wok or large skillet over medium-high heat. Add bacon and stir-fry for 3 to 4 minutes or just till crisp. Using a slotted spoon, remove cooked bacon from wok and drain on paper towels. Drain fat from wok.
1 tablespoon cooking oil 1 cup sliced fresh mushrooms 1 green onion, sliced	● Add oil to wok. (Add more oil as necessary during stir-frying.) Add mushrooms and green onion to wok. Stir-fry for 1 to 2 minutes in hot oil. Remove vegetables from the wok.
2 boneless, skinless chicken breast halves, cut into bite-size pieces (about ¾ pound)	● Add chicken to wok. Stir-fry for 2 to 3 minutes or till done. Add mushroom mixture and dressing mixture to wok. Heat mixture through.
3 cups torn romaine 3 cups torn leaf lettuce 3 hard-cooked eggs, cut into wedges	● Place greens and bacon in a large salad bowl. Pour hot mixture over greens and toss to coat. Top with egg wedges. Serve immediately. Makes 4 servings.

This meal-in-a-bowl salad may remind you of a wilted lettuce salad. All you need to complete the meal is some crusty bread and a bottle of wine.

Three-Ingredient Stir-Fry

1 tablespoon cooking oil 2 boneless, skinless chicken breast halves, cut into bite-size pieces (about ½ pound)	● Preheat a wok or large skillet over high heat. Add cooking oil. Stir-fry the chicken for 2 to 3 minutes or till done. Remove from wok.
1 10-ounce package frozen stir-fry vegetables with seasoning Hot cooked rice	● Stir-fry vegetables in wok or skillet according to package directions. Stir in chicken and heat through. Serve over rice. Makes 2 servings.

The frozen vegetables come already seasoned and salted.

Pork and Apple Stir-Fry

1 **pound boneless pork**	● Partially freeze pork. Thinly slice, across the grain, into bite-size pieces.	**Choose firm apples, such as Jonathan, McIntosh, or Granny Smith, for stir-frying. Softer apples break up when you cook them in your wok.**
¾ **cup apple juice or cider** 1 **tablespoon cornstarch** 1 **teaspoon instant beef bouillon granules** ½ **teaspoon ground cinnamon**	● For sauce, in a small bowl stir together the apple juice or cider, cornstarch, bouillon granules, and cinnamon. Set aside.	
1 **tablespoon cooking oil**	● Preheat a wok or large skillet over high heat. Add cooking oil. (Add more oil as necessary during stir-frying.) Add *half* of the pork to the wok or skillet. Stir-fry pork for 2 to 3 minutes or till done. Remove from wok. Stir-fry remaining pork for 2 to 3 minutes.	
2 **small apples, sliced into thin wedges** 6 **green onions, bias-sliced into 1-inch lengths** ⅓ **cups raisins** **Hot cooked rice**	● Return all pork to wok. Push meat from center of wok or skillet. Stir sauce and add to center of wok. Cook and stir till thickened and bubbly. Add apples, green onions, and raisins. Toss together and cook for 1 minute more. Serve with rice. Makes 4 servings.	

What's Partially Frozen Meat?

Many recipes in this book recommend that you partially freeze beef, pork, or lamb. This extra step firms the meat so it's easier to slice. Poultry products, link sausage, and fish slice easily without freezing.

   Our home economists suggest freezing meat just till firm (about 30 minutes) when you plan to slice it into bite-size pieces. For thin slicing, freeze the meat till partially frozen (45 to 60 minutes). If your meat is already frozen, let it thaw to the desired stage.

Ham and Pepper Stir-Fry

¼ cup water 2 tablespoons dry sherry 1 tablespoon cornstarch 1 tablespoon brown sugar 1 teaspoon chicken bouillon granules ½ teaspoon dry mustard	● For sauce, in a small mixing bowl stir together the water, dry sherry, cornstarch, brown sugar, chicken bouillon granules, and mustard. Set aside.

1 tablespoon cooking oil
2 cups fresh mushrooms,
   halved (about 3 cups)
1 green pepper, cut
   into bite-size pieces
1 medium onion, sliced and
   separated into rings
	● Preheat a wok or large skillet over high heat. Add cooking oil. (Add more oil as necessary during stir-frying.)
	   Stir-fry halved mushrooms, green pepper, and onion in hot oil for 3 to 4 minutes or till crisp-tender.

¾ pound fully cooked
   boneless ham slice, cut
   into bite-size strips
Hot cooked rice (optional)
	● Add ham to wok and heat through. Push ham and vegetables from center of wok or skillet.
	   Stir sauce and add to center of wok. Cook and stir till thickened and bubbly. Cook and stir for 2 minutes more. Serve with rice, if desired. Makes 4 servings.

The produce departments of some supermarkets offer sweet peppers in a variety of colors: yellow, red, purple, and green. Try combining two or three for a burst of color. The peppers all taste about the same.

Greek-Style Pitas

¾ pound boneless lamb *or* beef	● Partially freeze meat. Thinly slice, across the grain, into bite-size pieces.

1 tablespoon cooking oil
2 cloves garlic, minced
½ teaspoon dried oregano,
   crushed
¼ teaspoon dried thyme,
   crushed
	● Preheat a wok or large skillet over high heat. Add cooking oil. (Add more oil as necessary during stir-frying.)
	   Stir-fry the garlic, oregano, and thyme in hot oil for 30 seconds. Add lamb and stir-fry for 2 to 3 minutes or till done.

2 ounces feta cheese,
   crumbled
4 lettuce leaves
2 large pita bread rounds,
   halved crosswise
1 medium tomato, cut into
   thin slices
Plain yogurt
	● Add feta to wok or skillet and toss together over heat. Spoon mixture into lettuce-lined pita halves. Add tomato slices. Serve with dollops of yogurt. Makes 4 servings.

What better cheese to sprinkle on this sandwich than Greek feta. Made from sheep's milk, feta crumbles like blue cheese. If you can't find feta cheese, substitute crumbled farmer cheese.

Chocolate-Mint Mousse
(See recipe, page 41.)

Melon with Cream Fluff
(See recipe, page 40.)

Menu

California Stir-Fry
on rice

French Bread
with Garlic Butter

Melon with Cream Fluff

Chocolate-Mint Mousse

Coffee

Entertaining With a Stir-Fry

Company coming? How about an easy-to-fix stir-fry to headline your menu? We've planned this meal so all the other dishes are made before you warm up your wok. For added fun, invite everyone into your kitchen to help you stir-fry the main dish.

Menu

California Stir-Fry

French Bread with Garlic Butter

Melon with Cream Fluff

Chocolate-Mint Mousse

MENU COUNTDOWN

1 Day Ahead
● Prepare the Chocolate-Mint Mousse. Cover and chill overnight.

Several Hours Ahead
● Beat together the fluff for Melon with Cream Fluff. Cover; chill.
● Make chocolate curls to sprinkle over the dessert, if desired.

1 Hour Ahead
● Assemble and wrap French Bread with Garlic Butter in foil. Set aside.
● Cut up fruit for salad and arrange on plates. (If you use fruit that browns, cut it up at the last minute and brush with lemon juice.)

½ Hour Ahead
● Preheat the oven to 400° for the French bread.
● Stir together the sauce for California Stir-Fry. Cut up the ingredients.

20 Minutes Ahead
● Put the bread in the oven.
● Cook the rice for the stir-fry.

At Serving Time
● Whip the cream for the dessert and chill till serving time.
● Top the fruit with the cream fluff.
● Stir-fry the main dish.

California Stir-Fry

Pictured on page 36 and on the cover.

1 **teaspoon finely shredded orange peel** ⅔ **cup orange juice** 2 **tablespoons dry white wine** 1 **tablespoon cornstarch** ½ **teaspoon instant chicken bouillon granules**	● For sauce, in a small bowl stir together the orange peel, orange juice, white wine, cornstarch, and chicken bouillon granules. Set aside.
1 **tablespoon cooking oil** 1 **clove garlic, minced** 1 **medium sweet red *and/or* green pepper, cut into ¾-inch pieces**	● Preheat a wok or large skillet over high heat. Add cooking oil. (Add more oil as necessary during stir-frying.) Stir-fry garlic in hot oil for 30 seconds. Add pepper and stir-fry 1 to 2 minutes or till crisp-tender. Remove from wok.
4 **boneless, skinless chicken breast halves, cut into bite-size pieces (about 1 pound)**	● Stir-fry chicken, *half* at a time, for 2 to 3 minutes or till done. Return all chicken and vegetables to wok. Push from center of wok or skillet.
1 **medium avocado, peeled, pitted, and cut into ¾-inch chunks** ⅓ **cup sliced almonds** **Hot cooked rice**	● Stir sauce and add to center of wok. Cook and stir till thickened and bubbly. Add the avocado and almonds. Cook for 1 minute more. Serve over hot cooked rice. Makes 4 servings.

What do California and this stir-fry have in common? The ingredient list tells the story: orange peel and juice, peppers, an avocado, almonds, and wine—all California grown.

French Bread With Garlic Butter

Pictured on page 36.

1 **10- to 12-ounce loaf unsliced French bread** 3 **tablespoons margarine *or* butter, softened** ¼ **teaspoon garlic powder**	● Cut bread into 8 slices. Stir together the margarine or butter and garlic powder. Spread mixture between slices.
	● Wrap in foil. Bake in a 400° oven for 15 to 20 minutes or till heated through. Serve warm. Makes 4 servings.

If you know your guests love bread, make two loaves.

Melon with Cream Fluff

Pictured on page 37.

¼ cup soft-style cream cheese
¼ cup dairy sour cream
1 tablespoon honey
1 tablespoon milk
¼ teaspoon poppy seed (optional)

● In a small mixing bowl beat together the cream cheese, sour cream, honey, milk, and poppy seed, if desired. Cover and chill till serving time.

If melon is out of season, use whatever colorful fresh fruit you can find. Or, for an off-the-shelf solution, start with canned fruit.

1 medium cantaloupe *or* honeydew melon, seeded, and cut into 8 wedges
   Lettuce leaves
4 slices kiwi fruit

● Peel melon and arrange 2 melon wedges on each of 4 lettuce-lined plates. Dollop each serving with cheese mixture. Top with kiwi fruit. Makes 4 servings.

The Care And Feeding of Your Wok

With a little care, your wok will last for years.
● Scrub new carbon steel woks with cleanser and hot, soapy water to remove the rust-resistant coating. (If the lid is carbon steel, scrub it, too.) Let dry. Then, heat it on the range for a few minutes.

To season your wok, coat it with cooking oil. Heat it till very hot. Let the wok cool. Rub in oil. If the lid is carbon steel, season it, too. Remember to remove wooden handles before placing the lid directly over the burner on your range.

Clean and reseason your wok after each use. Soak the wok in plain hot water, then clean with a bamboo brush or loofah sponge. Rinse and dry. (Heat the wok on the range to dry.) Rub oil into the wok. Do the same for a carbon steel lid.
● Use a stainless steel or aluminum cleaner, as needed, for minimum-care woks, which are made with aluminum and stainless steel.
● Check manufacturer's care instructions for woks with nonstick coatings. For most nonstick coatings, clean surfaces thoroughly, dry, then rub with oil.

Thai Chicken Fried Rice

Pictured on page 60.

3 tablespoons fish sauce 1 teaspoon hot bean paste *or* hot bean sauce	● In a small bowl stir together the fish sauce and bean paste. Set aside.
1 tablespoon cooking oil 2 beaten eggs	● Preheat a wok or large skillet over medium-high heat. Add cooking oil. Add eggs. Lift and tilt the wok or skillet to form a thin sheet of egg 7 to 8 inches wide (see photos, page 58). Cook, without stirring, about 2 minutes or just till set. Slide egg sheet onto a cutting board. Cut into ¾-inch-wide strips. Cut strips into 2-inch lengths.
1 tablespoon cooking oil 2 cloves garlic, minced 1 medium onion, chopped 2 boneless, skinless chicken breast halves, cut into ½-inch cubes (about ½ pound)	● Return wok or skillet to high heat. Add cooking oil. (Add more oil as necessary during stir-frying.) Stir-fry the garlic and onion for 2 minutes. Add chicken and stir-fry for 2 to 3 minutes or till chicken is done.
3 cups chilled cooked rice	● Add the rice and fish sauce mixture. Stir for 1 minute or till heated through. Gently stir in the egg strips. Cover and cook for 1 minute.
2 tablespoons snipped cilantro *or* parsley 1 tablespoon lime juice 1 small tomato, cut into thin wedges 1 small cucumber, sliced Cilantro (optional)	● Add cilantro or parsley and lime juice. Toss lightly. Spoon onto a serving platter. Arrange tomato and cucumber around edge of platter. Garnish the dish with cilantro, if desired. Makes 6 to 8 side-dish servings.

In modern Thailand, people eat with a fork and a spoon, not chopsticks. As in the past, the traditional style of eating with the fingers also is practiced.

Thai Red Curry Pork

Thai Chicken Fried Rice
(See recipe, page 59.)

Thai Red Curry Pork

1 stalk fresh lemongrass, 1 tablespoon dried lemongrass, *or* 1 tablespoon finely shredded lemon peel	● For fresh lemongrass, remove and discard outer leaves and upper ⅔ of stalks. Thinly slice remaining stalk. For dried lemongrass, soak in enough warm water to cover for 2 hours, then drain and finely chop. Set aside.	**Lemongrass, serrano peppers, and fish sauce confirm this recipe's origin.**

1 pound boneless pork 10 dried mushrooms *or* one 4-ounce can sliced mushrooms, drained 2 cups fresh green beans cut into 1-inch lengths *or* one 9-ounce package frozen cut green beans	● Partially freeze pork. Thinly slice, across the grain, into bite-size pieces. For dried mushrooms, in a medium bowl combine mushrooms with enough warm water to cover. Let stand for 30 minutes. Drain well. Trim off stems and slice mushrooms. Set aside. If using fresh green beans, cook in a small amount of boiling water, covered, for 4 minutes; drain. (If using frozen beans, thaw.) Set aside.

Protect your hands with plastic bags or rubber gloves when cutting up chilies. Halve chilies and remove and discard seeds. The seeds contain most of the harsh oils.

1 *or* 2 fresh serrano chilies, seeded and cut into strips *or* finely chopped 4 teaspoons fish sauce 1 tablespoon water 1 teaspoon sugar	● In a small bowl combine chilies, fish sauce, water, and sugar. Set aside.

2 tablespoons cooking oil 1 tablespoon red curry paste	● Preheat a wok or large skillet. Add the cooking oil. (Add more oil as necessary during stir-frying.) Add fresh green beans to hot oil. Stir-fry green beans 2 minutes. Add lemongrass, soaked dried or canned mushrooms, and curry paste. Stir-fry for 1 to 2 minutes more. (If using frozen beans, add with lemongrass and mushrooms.) Remove from wok.

	● Add *half* of the pork and stir-fry for 2 to 3 minutes or till pork is done. Remove pork from wok and stir-fry remaining pork for 2 to 3 minutes. Return all meat and the green bean mixture to wok.

Cut the chilies into strips, then chop, if desired. Avoid direct contact with your eyes as you work. When finished, wash your hands thoroughly.

Hot cooked rice Sliced red chili pepper (optional)	● Push mixture from center of wok. Stir fish sauce mixture into center of wok. Stir-fry for 1 minute more. Serve with rice. Garnish with chili pepper, if desired. Makes 4 servings.

Philippine Noodles And Meat

½ **pound fresh** *or* **frozen peeled shrimp**	● Thaw shrimp, if frozen. Partially freeze pork. Thinly slice the pork, across the grain, into bite-size pieces. Cut chicken into bite-size pieces.
½ **pound boneless pork**	
2 **boneless, skinless chicken breast halves (about ½ pound)**	

Use all pork or all chicken with the peeled shrimp, if you like.

4 **ounces fresh** *or* **dried Chinese egg noodles** *or* **fine egg noodles**	● In a large saucepan cook egg noodles in a large amount of boiling water just till tender. (Cook fresh about 4 minutes or dried about 6 minutes.) Drain well and set noodles aside.

⅓ **cup water**	● For sauce, in a small mixing bowl stir together water, fish sauce, soy sauce, and pepper. Set aside.
2 **tablespoons fish sauce**	
1 **tablespoon soy sauce**	
¼ **teaspoon pepper**	

1 **tablespoon cooking oil**	● Preheat a wok or 12-inch skillet over high heat. Add cooking oil. (Add more oil as necessary during stir-frying.) Stir-fry garlic and onions for 1 minute. Add Chinese cabbage and stir-fry for 1 minute. (For regular cabbage, stir-fry 3 minutes.) Remove vegetables from wok.
2 **cloves garlic, minced**	
2 **medium onions, chopped**	
4 **cups shredded Chinese cabbage** *or* **regular cabbage**	

1 **lemon, cut into wedges**	● Stir-fry chicken for 2 to 3 minutes or till done. Remove from wok. Stir-fry pork for 2 to 3 minutes. Remove from wok. Stir-fry shrimp for 2 to 3 minutes. Return chicken and pork to wok.

Be sure each person squeezes some lemon juice over his or her serving for added tang.

	● Push mixture from center of wok. Add sauce. Cook and stir till bubbly. Add noodles and vegetables to wok. Cover and cook the mixture for 1 minute. Arrange on a serving platter. Serve with lemon. Makes 6 servings.

Vietnamese Beef and Potato Stir-Fry

1 pound beef top round steak	● Partially freeze beef. Thinly slice, across the grain, into bite-size pieces.
½ cup water **2 tablespoons fish sauce** **2 teaspoons cornstarch**	● For sauce, in a small mixing bowl stir together water, fish sauce, and cornstarch. Set aside.
1 tablespoon cooking oil **1½ cups frozen shoestring French fries, thawed**	● Preheat a wok or large skillet over high heat. Add oil. (Add more oil as necessary during stir-frying.) 　Add the thawed French fries and stir-fry for 2 to 3 minutes or till golden. Remove from wok.
4 cloves garlic, minced **1 medium onion, cut into 8 wedges** **1 medium green pepper, cut into 1-inch pieces**	● Add garlic to wok and stir-fry for 30 seconds. Add onion wedges and stir-fry for 1 minute. 　Add green pepper and stir-fry about 2 minutes more or till vegetables are crisp-tender. Remove from wok.
	● Add *half* of the beef to wok. Stir-fry for 2 to 3 minutes or till done. Remove from wok. Stir-fry remaining beef for 2 to 3 minutes. Return all meat to wok.
1 small tomato, cut into thin wedges	● Push meat from center of wok or skillet. Stir sauce; add to center of wok or skillet. Cook and stir till mixture is thickened and bubbly. 　Add potatoes, onion, and green pepper. Heat through. Fold in tomato wedges. Makes 4 servings.

The traditional Vietnamese recipe starts with fresh potatoes that you peel, slice, and fry. We've eliminated all those steps without changing the flavor by substituting frozen French fries. It's a real meat-and-potatoes main dish.

Electric wok

Stir-fry pan

Classic round-bottomed wok

Take a Wok

Get yourself a wok or a skillet and a long-handled stirrer, and you're ready to stir-fry. What type of wok should you choose? You'll find some of your options on these two pages.

Woks vary in diameter and volume. The most common is the 14- to 16-inch wok—perfect for two to four servings.

The classic round-bottomed wok needs a ring stand to support it. For an electric range, turn up the wide side of the ring stand so the wok sits closer to the heating unit. For a gas range, elevating the wok actually places it over a hotter part of the gas flame.

Place the ring stand over the largest burner with the narrow side up.

The flat-bottomed wok fits the electric range best because it sits right on the heating unit. You won't need a ring. Some cookware manufacturers have **stir-fry pans** in their lines. A stir-fry pan looks and cooks like a flat-bottomed wok. It's handy for everyday frying, too.

The biggest advantage of **electric woks** is their portability. You can stir-fry right at the table for added fun. Sometimes the food takes longer to cook as the wok's thermostat cycles on and off, but the food still tastes great. Read the manufacturer's directions for basic information on using and caring for electric woks.

If you like, substitute a large **skillet** for a wok when stir-frying. In most cases, a 10-inch skillet will be large enough. For more than 4 cups of ingredients, you need the larger, 12-inch skillet.

For more information, see *The Care and Feeding of Your Wok,* page 40.

Flat-bottomed wok

Skillet

Wokking Chef's Salad

⅓ cup cooking oil
⅓ cup tarragon vinegar *or* vinegar
¼ teaspoon salt
¼ teaspoon pepper

● For dressing, in a small mixing bowl stir together the oil, vinegar, salt, and pepper. Set aside.

---

1 tablespoon cooking oil
1 clove garlic, minced
1 green onion, thinly sliced
2 boneless, skinless chicken breast halves, cut into bite-size strips (8 ounces)

● Preheat a wok or 12-inch skillet over high heat. Add cooking oil. (Add more oil as necessary during stir-frying.)
   Stir-fry garlic and onion 30 seconds. Add chicken and stir-fry for 2 minutes.

---

4 ounces fully cooked ham, cut into bite-size strips

● Add ham and stir-fry for 1 to 2 minutes or till chicken is done. Add dressing mixture to wok and heat through. Remove wok from heat.

---

1 cup sliced fresh mushrooms
⅓ cup sunflower nuts

● Add sliced mushrooms and nuts to wok or skillet. Toss mixture.

---

6 cups torn mixed greens
4 ounces cheddar cheese, cut into ½-inch cubes
4 ounces Swiss cheese, cut into ½-inch cubes

● Add greens and cheese to wok. Toss to mix. Makes 4 or 5 servings.

Here's a chef's salad with a difference: It's served hot from your wok. Heat the meat and vegetables in your wok. Then, drizzle on dressing and toss with the greens. Serve the salad right away.

Chicken and Chili Tacos

1	4-ounce can diced green chili peppers
2	tablespoons salsa
½	teaspoon cornstarch

● For sauce, in a small bowl stir together *undrained* chili peppers, salsa, and cornstarch. Set aside.

For those who like it hot, make the tacos with hot green chili peppers and hot-style salsa instead of the milder choices.

1	tablespoon cooking oil
1	clove garlic, minced
1	teaspoon chili powder
½	teaspoon ground cumin

● Preheat a wok or large skillet over high heat. Add cooking oil. (Add more oil as necessary during stir-frying.) Stir-fry garlic, chili powder, and ground cumin in hot oil for 30 seconds.

| 4 | boneless, skinless chicken breast halves, cut into bite-size pieces (about 1 pound) |

● Add *half* of the chicken to the wok. Stir-fry chicken for 2 to 3 minutes or till done. Remove chicken from wok.

Stir-fry remaining chicken for 2 to 3 minutes. Return all chicken to wok.

	Dash salt
8	taco shells
1	cup shredded Colby-Monterey Jack cheese (4 ounces)
1	cup shredded lettuce Salsa Chopped tomato (optional) Dairy sour cream (optional)

● Stir green chili mixture into chicken. Cook and stir for 2 minutes more. Sprinkle lightly with salt. Divide meat mixture between taco shells.

Top with cheese, then lettuce and salsa. Top with chopped tomato and sour cream, if desired. Makes 4 servings.

Speedy Rice

For fast rice, combine 1½ cups quick-cooking rice with 1½ cups boiling water for 2⅔ cups cooked rice—about 4 servings.

Cook the rice just before you start stir-frying. Then, cover and remove the rice from the heat. Let it stand for at least 5 minutes as you finish stir-frying.